My
about God

Carine Mackenzie

CF4·K

10 9 8 7 6 5 4 3 2 1
© Copyright 2013 Carine Mackenzie
ISBN: 978-1-78191-260-7
Published by
Christian Focus Publications,
Geanies House, Fearn,
Ross-shire, IV20 1TW, U.K.

Scripture quotations are based on The Holy Bible, English
Standard Version, copyright © 2001 by Crossway Bibles,
a division of Good News Publishers. Used by permission.
All rights reserved. ESV Text Edition: 2007.

www.christianfocus.com
E-mail: info@christianfocus.com

Cover design by Alister MacInnes and
Daniel van Straaten
All illustrations by Diane Mathes

Printed and bound by Bell and Bain, Glasgow

Contents

Introduction

GOD – this is a big subject. Where do we start? God has no beginning and no end and is so great that our minds cannot fully grasp him. That does not mean that we should not think about him. He wants us to do that. He delights in us worshipping him. That is what we are made for.

God helps us to do this by telling us about himself in the Bible and in this little book we will look at some of the things that God has told us about himself.

Carine Mackenzie

1. God

I am the LORD and there is no other, besides me there is no God.
Isaiah 45:5

God is a Spirit. He does not have a body like we have. We cannot see him, but he is very real. God is great and powerful - more than we can understand.

God had no beginning as we had. He has no end either. God never changes. He was and is and always will be wise, holy, true and loving.

There is only one living and true God - he is the greatest and the best.

2. The Trinity

Go therefore and make disciples of all nations, baptising them in the name of the Father and of the Son and of the Holy Spirit.
Matthew 28:19

The Bible tells us there is only one God. It tells us of three different persons in this one God - God the Father, God the Son and God the Holy Spirit. These three persons are each God. They are equal in power and glory, but they each do different things.

3. God the Father

(Jesus said), Pray then like this:
'Our Father in heaven, hallowed
be your name.'
Matthew 6:9

God the Father lives in heaven, but
he is everywhere.

God the Father chooses and calls his people to be saved.

God the Father sent his Son to be the Saviour.

Jesus prayed to God the Father and taught us to pray to him too.

4. God the Son

For God so loved the world, that he gave his only Son, that whoever believes in him should not perish but have eternal life.
John 3:16

God the Son was sent by the Father to this world. He was born to Mary and was given the name **Jesus** which means 'The Lord Saves'.

Jesus was a human like us, but he was also God. Because he was God and man, he was able to be the perfect sacrifice for our sins when he died on the cross.

5. God the Holy Spirit

Likewise the Spirit helps us in our weakness. For we do not know what to pray for as we ought, but the Spirit himself intercedes for us with groanings too deep for words.
Romans 8:26

God the Holy Spirit is given to God's people by the Father and the Son, to live within them.

The Holy Spirit helps us to pray, helps us to understand the Bible, helps us to love and trust in the Lord Jesus Christ.

When someone becomes a Christian, they are 'born again' or 'born of the Spirit'. The Lord Jesus taught us this.

6. God is Infinite

Can you find out the deep things of God? Can you find out the limit of the Almighty? It is higher than heaven – what can you do?
Job 11:7-8

There is no limit to God and his power. There is a limit to what we can do, but not with God.

There is no limit to his love. He loves with an everlasting love – no beginning and no end. Our love at best is very faint in comparison.

There is no limit to God's goodness, or wisdom or justice or truth.

God is infinite – no limits. Our minds, which are limited, find this hard to grasp, but we should believe and worship him as the infinite God.

7. God is Eternal/ Everlasting

From everlasting to everlasting you are God.
Psalm 90:2

We live in a certain time in history. The calendar and the clock affect our daily lives. God is not affected by time. God is eternal. He had no beginning. He has no end. He inhabits eternity which is not confined by time. With God, a day is like a thousand years, and a thousand years like a day.

God has promised eternal life to those who trust in the Lord Jesus Christ, the Saviour from sin.

8. God is Unchanging

For I the LORD do not change.
Malachi 3:6

We are always changing. Our appearance changes as we grow older. Our tastes change. Our work changes. The seasons and the weather changes.

God never changes. He remains the same constantly. His promises never change. His plans and purposes never change.

He is the same yesterday and today and forever.

9. God is Immortal

To the King of the ages, immortal, invisible, the only God, be honor and glory forever and ever. Amen.
1 Timothy 1:17

God is immortal because he never dies. People die, as do animals and

birds and flowers and leaves. God's immortality is part of his nature.

He has given his people a gift – a soul that never dies and the promise of eternal life in heaven with himself.

10. God is Invisible

(God) who is the blessed and only Sovereign, the King of kings and Lord of lords ... whom no one has ever seen or can see.
1 Timothy 6:15-16

God is invisible because he is a Spirit. God can see us all the time.

We cannot see the wind, but we can see the effects of the wind blowing the trees or making the sea rough.

We can see the effects of God at work in the world that he made and in the way he keeps us and provides for us.

11. God is Omnipotent/ Almighty

The LORD appeared to Abram and said to him, 'I am God Almighty, walk before me, and be blameless.'
Genesis 17:1

All power in heaven and in earth belongs to God. He alone has the

power to give life and breath to every creature. The most powerful man in the world is feeble compared to the powerful God. Nobody can resist God and his purposes.

God even has power to forgive sin.

12. God is Omnipresent/ Everywhere

'Can a man hide himself in secret places so that I cannot see him?' declares the LORD. 'Do I not fill heaven and earth?' declares the LORD.
Jeremiah 23:24

God is omnipresent. We can be in only one place at one time. God is a Spirit. He does not have a body. He

is everywhere. He fills the whole earth and heaven.

He is with us when we are awake or asleep. He is with us at home, at play, at church and at school. He is with us when we are happy or sad. There is no place at all where God is not present.

13. God is Omniscient/ All-knowing

For he (God) knows the secrets of the heart.
Psalm 44:21

God knows everything. He even knows the number of hairs on your head. He knows when a little bird falls to the ground. He knows how many stars are in the sky. He knows what we say, and do and think about.

God knows all things. He knows if we love him.

14. God's Work of Creation

In the beginning, God created the heavens and the earth.
Genesis 1:1

God made the world and everything in it in six days. He made it from nothing, just by speaking his powerful word. He made the sun, the moon and all the stars. He made the day and the night. He made the birds, the fish and the animals. God formed a man called Adam from the dust of the ground and breathed life into him. God put Adam to sleep and removed one of his ribs. God created a woman called Eve from Adam's rib.

God was pleased with all that he had made - his work of Creation.

15. God's Work of Providence

(God) works all things according to the counsel of his will.
Ephesians 1:11

God's power not only made the world and everything in it, but keeps it going every day. God is the

sustainer of all life. He is good and kind and in control of all things. Nothing takes him by surprise.

All events in our lives happen to fulfil his purpose – even the things that we think are sad or difficult. His ways are far above our ways. He has a plan for all his people – a plan for our good and his glory.

16. God is Holy

Holy, holy, holy is the LORD of hosts; the whole earth is full of his glory.
Isaiah 6:3

God is completely free from sin. This means he is so different from us, because we sin in what we think,

and say and do. Because God is holy, he hates sin and has to punish it. The Saviour, Jesus Christ, God's Son took the punishment for those who believe in him.

God asks his people to be holy as he is holy. This is a gradual work of God's grace - not complete until death.

Because God is holy, we should worship him.

17. God is Good

For the L<small>ORD</small> is good; his steadfast love endures forever, and his faithfulness to all generations.
Psalm 100:5

God is good in all that he is and all that he does. He is good when he

gives us so many good gifts - food, drink, shelter, family.

He is good because he keeps his promises. He is good because he gave us wise commandments to follow. He is good when he corrects us for our mistakes. He is so good to us because he gave us his Son and will graciously give us all things.

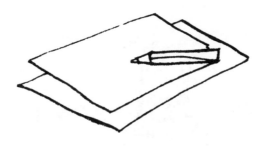

18. God is Righteous

The LORD within her is righteous; he does no injustice.
Zephaniah 3:5

God is righteous and just. He never does wrong. He never makes a mistake.

He is the Judge and all his judgements are always completely fair and just.

We do not always understand what God is doing in the world or in our lives, but we can be confident that he understands and is doing everything fairly and wisely.

19. God is Gracious

The LORD is gracious and merciful, slow to anger and abounding in steadfast love.
Psalm 145:8

Grace is the undeserved love of God to people because of what Jesus Christ has done.

All that God does for us is because he is gracious and deals with us, not because we deserve his love and favour, but because he delights in love and mercy. He is also absolutely just and hates sin, but Jesus Christ, the Son of God has taken the punishment for the sin of his people.

If God gave us what we deserve, we would be destroyed. But God is more gracious than we can understand. How thankful we should be.

20. God is Love

God is love, and whoever abides in love abides in God and God abides in him.
1 John 4:16

God does not only *show* love to his people, he *is* love. Love is one of

his main characteristics. We may love someone who is good to us, but God loved us even when we were his enemies. His love is so great it reaches the heavens, David the psalm-writer said (Psalm 36:5).

He loved us so much that he sent his Son to die for us on the cross. There is no greater love than that. The Bible tells us that we love because God first loved us.

21. God is True

But the LORD is the true God; he is the loving God and the everlasting King.
Jeremiah 10:10

The LORD God is the only true God. Many people in the world worship

false gods, an idol of stone or a person or an idea. These false gods cannot hear or answer prayer.

God's character is true. He does not lie. All he says is the truth. We can completely rely on him and his Word.

22. God Guides

This is God, our God forever and ever. He will guide us forever.
Psalm 48:14

When we are on a journey it is good to have a guide to point us in the

right direction, so that we do not stray off the road and into danger.

Life is like a journey and God is the best guide we can have. His Word tells us how to live in obedience and love to him and how to serve and love other people.

God guides us in the things which happen from day to day.

23. God Teaches

I will instruct you and teach you in the way you should go.
Psalm 32:8

Our teachers at school will tell us about many subjects – maths, geography, history. We have to listen and be willing to learn.

God, in his Word, teaches us about himself, about the dangers of sin, about the salvation that has been obtained for us by the Lord Jesus Christ. How important it is to pay attention and learn these valuable lessons.

God teaches us by his 'providence' in the things that happen to us day by day. Even the hard and difficult happenings teach us good lessons. God does all things well.

24. God Corrects

The LORD reproves (or corrects) him whom he loves, as a father the son in whom he delights.
Proverbs 3:12

When we make a mistake in a school exercise, the teacher will point out

the mistake and help us to reach the correct answer.

God hates sin. When his people sin, God as a loving Father, must point out that sin and correct them.

God, in his Word, confronts us with our sin and shows us the correct way to think and act.

If we confess our sin, he is faithful and just to forgive us our sin.

25. God Comforts

Blessed be the God and Father of our Lord Jesus Christ, the Father of mercies and God of all comfort, who comforts us in all our affliction.
2 Corinthians 1:3-4

If our friend is unhappy or in trouble, we sometimes do not

know what to say to help them. We might say something that only makes them feel worse. But God always knows how to comfort. His love is perfect. He is the God of all comfort. His words encourage and strengthen us when we are unhappy or in trouble.

'Do not let your hearts be troubled,' he tells us. 'Believe in God.' The Bible is full of comforting words like that.

26. God is Forgiving

If we confess our sins, he is faithful and just to forgive us our sins and to cleanse us from all unrighteousness.
1 John 1:9

Only God can forgive sin. He cancels the sinner's debt because Jesus Christ, God's Son, died on the cross

to bear the punishment for the sin of those who repent and trust in him.

God has promised that when he forgives their iniquity, he will not remember their sin any more. Micah told us that God will cast all our sin into the depths of the sea. God delights to forgive the sinner who comes to him in faith.

27. God is King

For God is the King of all the earth; sing praises with a psalm.
Psalm 47:7

A king is a ruler of a kingdom and is the most important person in

the country. God is the King over everyone in the world, even all the kings and queens and presidents. He is the King of kings, and Lord of lords. His kingdom will last for ever.

The Bible tells us that one day everyone in the world will bow down before him and worship.

28. God gave his Word

All Scripture is breathed out by God and profitable for teaching, for reproof, for correction and for training in righteousness.
2 Timothy 3:16

How we love to receive a letter or a card from someone we love. We like to know that they are thinking of us.

God has sent us an amazing message – not just one letter – but in the sixty-six books of the Bible, telling us that he is thinking of us and loves us. He tells us about himself and what he has done for us. He tells us what we are to believe and what we are to do.

God's book has survived down through the centuries. 'Heaven and earth will disappear,' Jesus the Son of God said, 'but my words will remain for ever.'

29. God gives all Things

He who did not spare his own Son, but gave him up for us all, how will he not also with him graciously give us all things?
Romans 8:32

We all need food and clothes and a home. Our parents provide these

for us, probably. But it is God who has provided, so that your needs will be met. All good gifts come from him.

Our need for love, security, protection come first from God our Heavenly Father. He cares for us more than anyone else could. Nothing is too hard for him. He does not promise to supply everything we *want*, but we can depend on him to supply all our *needs*.

30. God's Name

I will praise the name of God with a song; I will magnify him with thanksgiving.
Psalm 69:30

One of the commandments tells us not to take God's name in vain. We must use his name with care and reverence.

God has many special names which tell us about his character.

Elohim tells us that he is strong and mighty.

Jehovah Jireh reminds us that he provides for all our needs.

El Elyon means Most High.

Yahweh is a very personal, holy, name which God uses with his special people. They can use the name **Yahweh** because God made a covenant (a special promise) with them, promising to be their faithful God.

31. We are made to Worship God

All the ends of the earth shall remember and turn to the LORD, and all the families of the nations shall worship before you.
Psalm 22:27

The bird is made to fly. The fish is made to swim. And we are made to worship God.

Our chief purpose in living is to serve God who made us. Everything we do should be to the glory of God – eating, drinking, playing, working. Worshipping in church is just a part of serving him.

From the Author

Our chief purpose in life is to glorify God and enjoy him forever. God has revealed to us so much of his character and work in creation and providence and the Bible to help us to do this.

We will never grasp the great extent of his being, but we can enjoy the little that we do understand. We cannot see the beauty and wonder of the whole world, but we can enjoy even the view of the garden from the kitchen window or simply the little bird in the sky.

I pray that as you use this little book, you will see something of the wonder, majesty and glory of God. May this book help you to thank God for what he has told you about himself and then you will glorify and enjoy him.

Carine Mackenzie

OTHER BOOKS IN THE SERIES

My 1st Book of Bible Prayers, Philip Ross
ISBN: 978-1-85792-944-7

My 1st Book of Bible Promises, Carine Mackenzie
ISBN: 978-1-84550-039-9

My 1st Book of Christian Values, Carine Mackenzie
ISBN: 978-1-84550-262-1

My 1st Book of Memory Verses, Carine Mackenzie
ISBN: 978-1-85792-783-2

My 1st Book about the Church, Carine Mackenzie
ISBN: 978-1-84550-570-7

My 1st Book of Questions and Answers,
Carine Mackenzie
ISBN: 978-1-85792-570-8

My 1st Book about Jesus, Carine Mackenzie
ISBN: 978-1-84550-463-2

My 1st Book about the Bible, Carine Mackenzie
ISBN: 978-1-78191-123-5

CHRISTIAN FOCUS PUBLICATIONS

Christian Focus Christian Heritage CF4K Mentor

Christian Focus Publications publishes books for adults and children under its four main imprints: Christian Focus, CF4K, Mentor and Christian Heritage. Our books reflect our conviction that God's Word is reliable and Jesus is the way to know him, and live for ever with him.

Our children's publication list includes a Sunday School curriculum that covers pre-school to early teens, and puzzle and activity books. We also publish personal and family devotional titles, biographies and inspirational stories that children will love.

If you are looking for quality Bible teaching for children then we have an excellent range of Bible stories and age-specific theological books.

From pre-school board books to teenage apologetics, we have it covered!

Find us at our web page:
www.christianfocus.com

CF4•K
Because you're never
too young to know Jesus